1000 SIGHT WORDS THE ULTIMATE VOCABULARY BOOK

PICTURE DICTIONARY WITH SENTENCE

English - Vietnamese

action

hành động

Action!

actually

thực ra

I actually like strawberry.

adjective

tính từ

Tell me an adjective to describe this.

afraid

sợ

What are you afraid of?

agreed

đã đồng ý

They agreed on music.

ahead

phía trước

Who was ahead in the race?

allow

cho phép

Did the teacher allow him to go play?

apple

táo

Eat an apple.

arrived

đã đến

My plane arrived on time.

born

sinh ra

Where were you born?

bought

đã mua

She bought new clothes.

British

người anh

Who is the British monarch?

capital

thủ đô

The capital is in Washington DC.

chance

cơ hội

Dice is a game of chance.

chart

đồ thị

What does your medical chart say?

church

nhà thờ

Did you go to church?

column

cột

Did you read the newspaper column?

company

công ty

What company do you work for?

conditions

điều kiện

What are the weather conditions.

corn

ngô

Do you like corn?

cotton

bông

A q-tip is made of cotton.

cows

bò

How many cows does he have?

create

tạo nên

What art did you create?

dead

đã chết

The bug is dead.

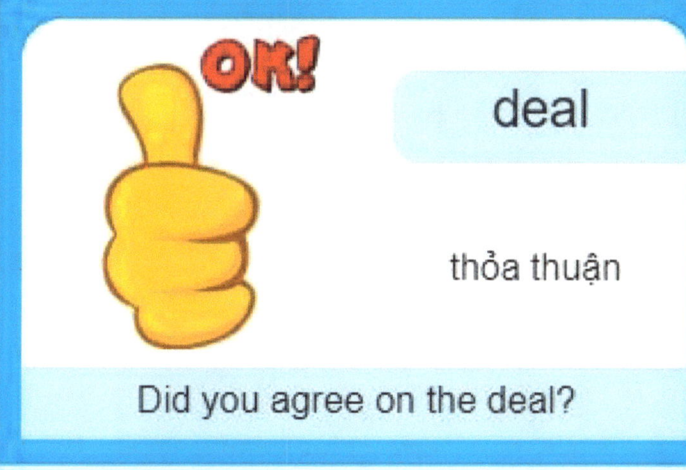

deal

thỏa thuận

Did you agree on the deal?

death

tử vong

The grim reaper is death.

details

chi tiết

Look for the details.

determine

mục đích

Did you determine where to go eat?

difficult

khó khăn

I found this difficult.

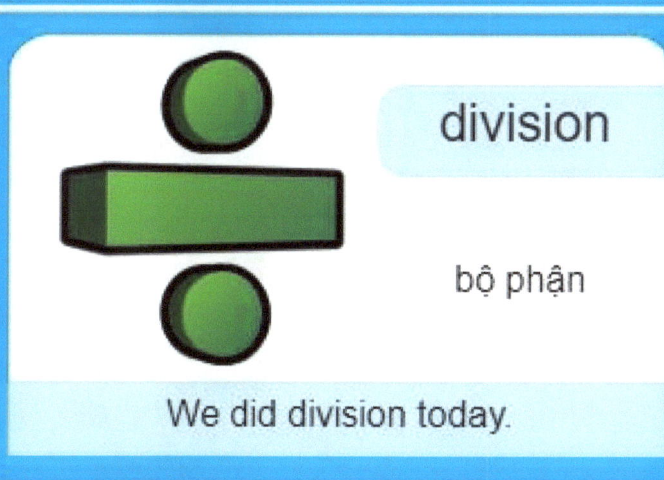

division

bộ phận

We did division today.

doesn't

không phải

Doesn't it sound beautiful?

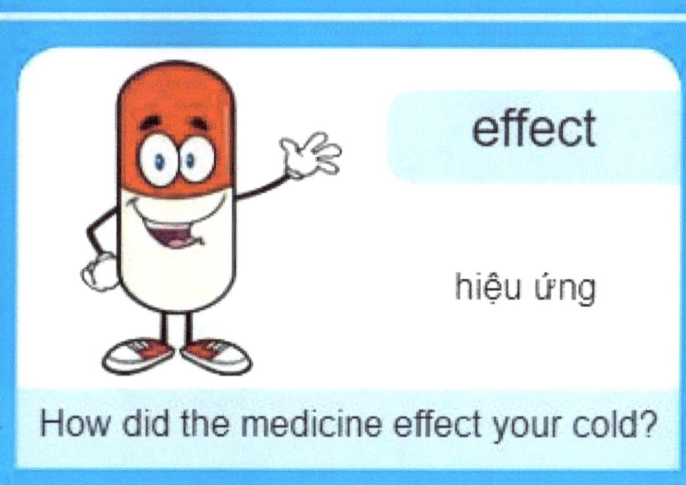

effect

hiệu ứng

How did the medicine effect your cold?

entire

toàn bộ

The entire family was in the picture.

especially

đặc biệt

She especially liked writing.

evening

tối

The ceremony was this evening.

experience

kinh nghiệm

She has a lot of experience.

factories

nhà máy

There are a lot of factories there.

fair

công viên vui vẻ

Let's go to the fair.

fear

nỗi sợ

I have a huge fear of clowns.

fig

quả sung

I ate a fig.

forward

ở đằng trước

Spring forward the clocks.

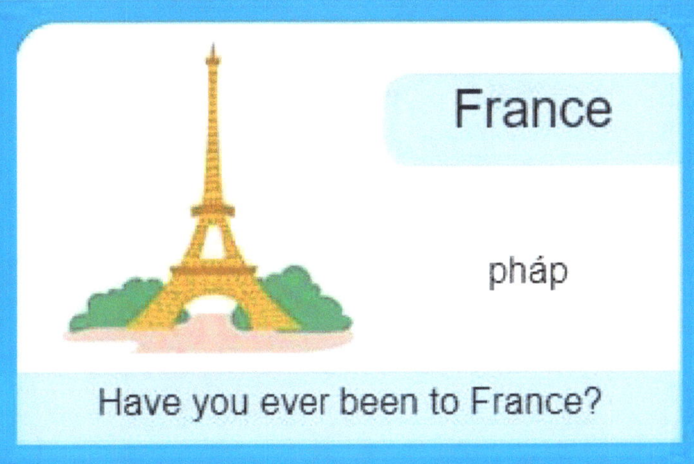

France

pháp

Have you ever been to France?

fresh

tươi

All the fruit is fresh.

Greek

người hy lạp

Have you ever had Greek food?

gun

súng

We played with a water gun.

hoe

cuốc

Use a hoe in the garden.

huge

khổng lồ

Those trees are huge!

isn't

không phải

Isn't it nice to hang out with friends?

led

lãnh đạo

The dog led her.

level

cấp độ

Use the level to hang the picture.

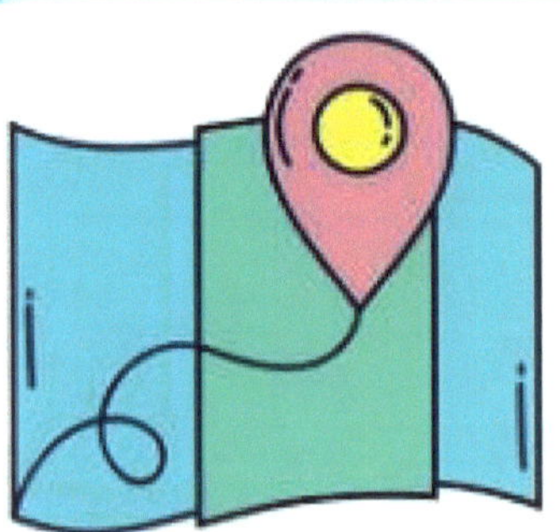

located

nằm

Where is the store located?

march

diễn hành

Are you going to march with the band?

match

phù hợp

Did you match them?

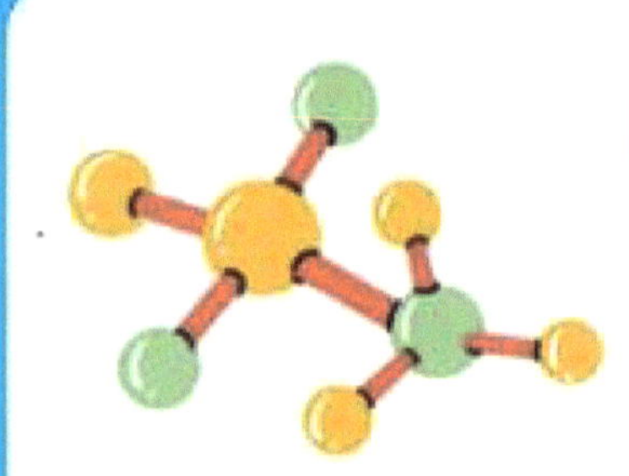

molecules

phân tử

Are those molecules?

northern

bắc

He lives in northern California.

nose

mũi

My nose is running.

office
văn phòng

Do you need any office supplies?

oxygen
ôxy

What is the symbol for oxygen?

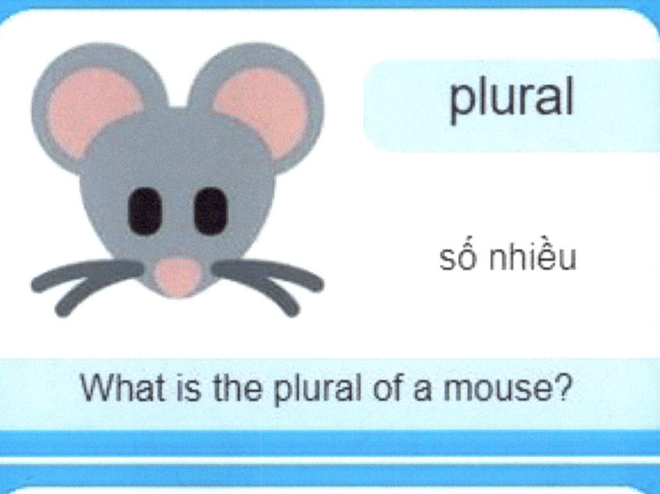

plural
số nhiều

What is the plural of a mouse?

prepared
chuẩn bị

She prepared for the exam.

pretty
đẹp

Pretty in pink.

printed
in

She printed out the forms.

radio
đài

Let's listen to the radio.

repeated
nói lại

They repeated the exercises daily.

rope

dây thừng

Do you have any rope?

rose

hoa hồng

Thank you for the rose.

score

ghi bàn

What was the final score?

seat

ghế

The girls took a seat in the sand.

settled

định cư

The case was settled.

shoes

giày

Put your shoes on.

shop

cửa hàng

I'm need to go shop for groceries.

similar

giống

The halves are similar.

sir
quý ngài
Yes, sir!

sister
em gái
Is she your sister?

smell
mùi
I love the smell of cookies!

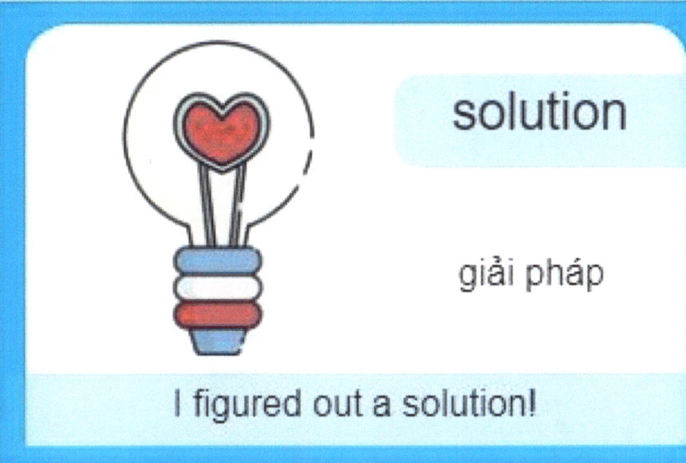

solution
giải pháp
I figured out a solution!

southern
miền nam
She's a southern belle.

steel
thép
The new building used steel.

stretched
kéo dài
We stretched before the workout.

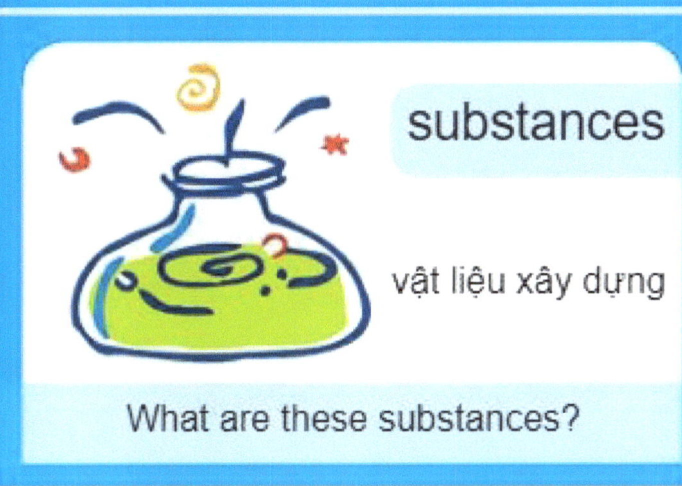

substances
vật liệu xây dựng
What are these substances?

suffix

hậu tố

What is the suffix of the word?

sugar

đường

Sugar cube for your tea?

tools

công cụ

May I borrow your tools?

total

toàn bộ

What's the total?

track

theo dõi

The runners got on the track.

triangle

tam giác

How many sides does a triangle have?

truck

xe tải

Is thaty our truck?

underline

underline

gạch chân

Underline the word.

various

đa dạng

I watch various shows.

view

lượt xem

That is a beautiful view!

Washington

washington

She is from Washington.

we'll

sẽ

We'll finish buying our groceries.

western

miền tây

It's western wear day.

win

thắng lợi

Did you win?

woman

đàn bà

The woman was on her way to work.

workers

công nhân

The workers were busy.

wouldn't

không phải

Wouldn't you like to go shopping?

wrong

sai lầm

Did I get it wrong?

yellow

màu vàng

A banana is yellow.

after

sau

You may have dessert after dinner.

again

lần nữa

May we go on the ride again?

air

không khí

The air was cold.

also

cũng thế

I also like baseball.

America

mỹ

Columbus sailed to America.

animal
động vật
My favorite animal is a lion.

another
khác
Have another cookie.

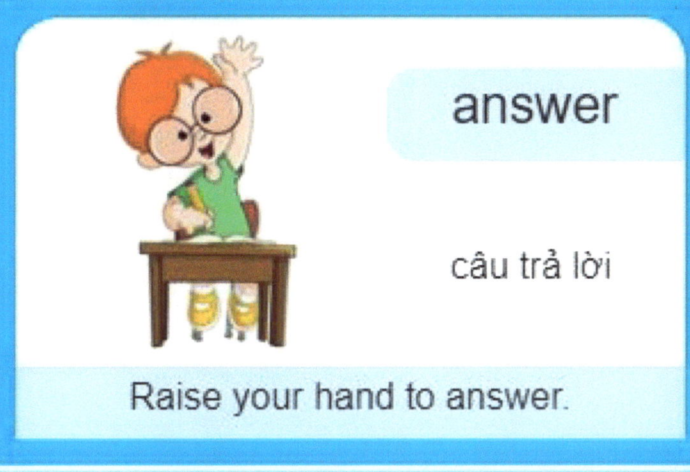

answer
câu trả lời
Raise your hand to answer.

any
bất kì
Do you have any crayons?

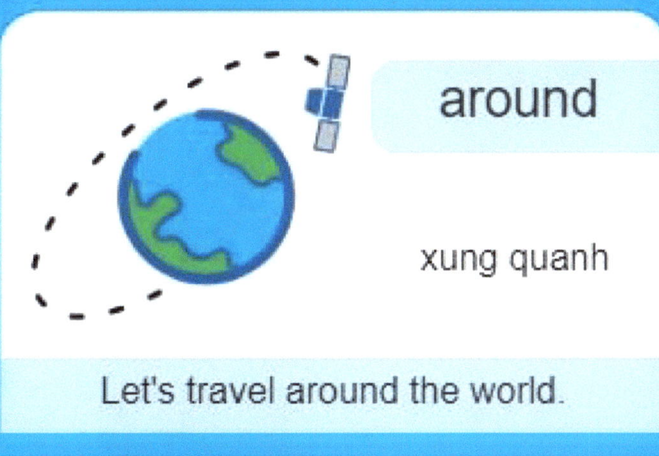

around
xung quanh
Let's travel around the world.

ask
hỏi
It's good to ask questions.

away
xa
Throw your trash away.

back
trở lại
We went back to school.

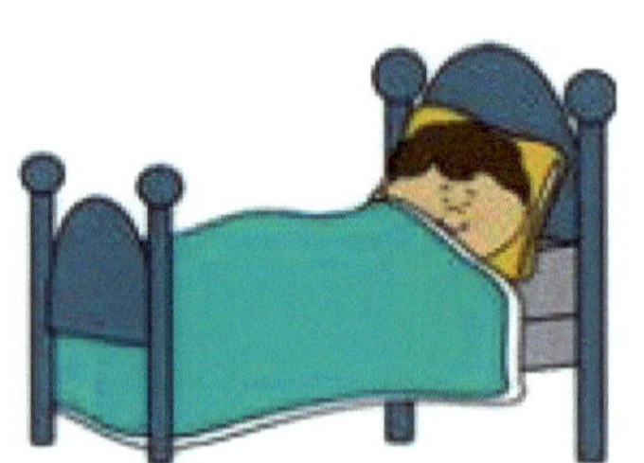

because

bởi vì

I went to bed because I was tired.

before

trước

Sharpen your pencil before the test.

big

lớn

The elephant is a big animal.

boy

con trai

The boy played a basketball.

came

đã đến

He came to class.

change

thay đổi

I save my change.

different

khác nhau

They use different balls.

does

làm

Does he ride the bus?

end

kết thúc

She watched to the end.

even

cũng

They learned about even numbers.

follow

theo

Follow the teacher.

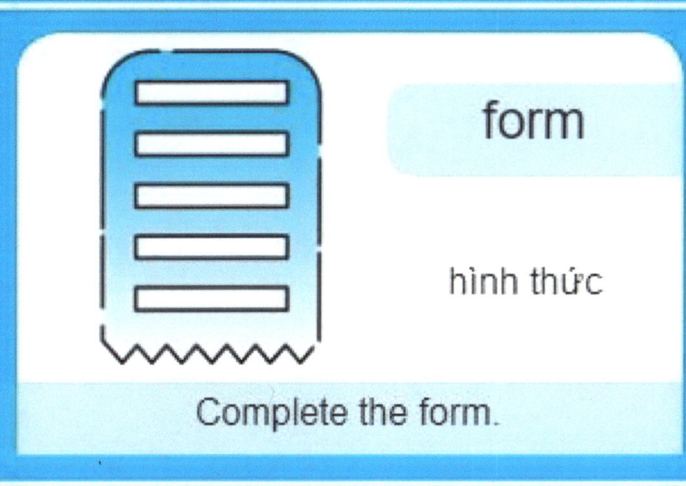

form

hình thức

Complete the form.

found

tìm

We found a puppy.

give

đưa cho

I like to give gifts.

good

tốt

The hamburger was good.

great

tuyệt quá

Great job!

hand

tay

Please hand in your work.

help

cứu giúp

You should help others.

here

đây

Do you sit here?

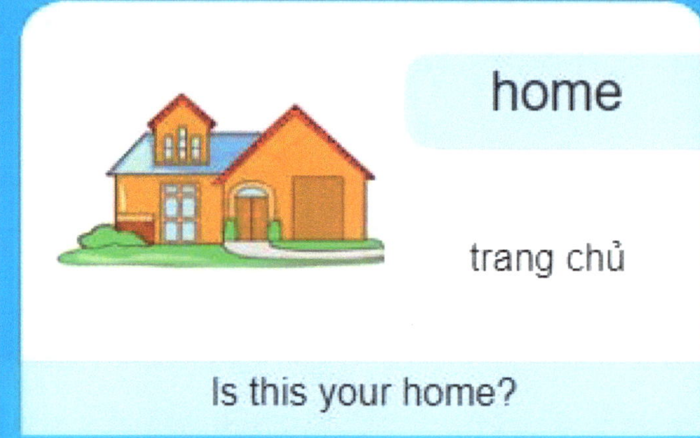

home

trang chủ

Is this your home?

house

nhà ở

The doll house was pink.

just

chỉ

The train just left.

kind

tử tế

Be kind to each other.

know

biết rồi

I don't know.

land

đất

They bought some land.

large

lớn

A bear is large.

learn

học hỏi

It's fun to learn science.

letter

lá thư

He mailed a letter.

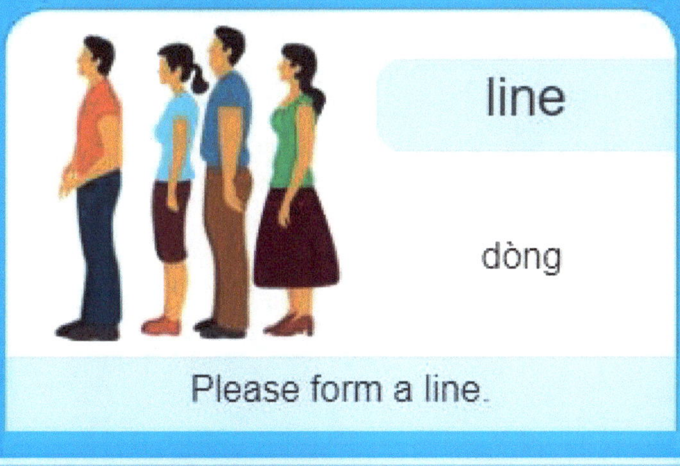

line

dòng

Please form a line.

little

ít

He has a little sister.

live

trực tiếp

You live in the city.

man

đàn ông

The man drove.

me

tôi

Come with me to the park.

means

có nghĩa

She got her by means of a taxi.

men

đàn ông

The men played football.

most

phần lớn

Most students like to help.

mother

mẹ

He loves his mother.

move

di chuyển

His family decided to move.

much

nhiều

How much is the camera?

must

phải

You must raise your hand.

name

tên

What is his name?

need

muốn

Do you need to sleep?

new

mới

We have a new teacher.

off

tắt

The rocket blasted off.

old

cũ

Those are old toys.

only

chỉ có

There's only one slice left.

our

của chúng tôi

She was our teacher.

over

kết thúc

He jumped over it.

Please turn the page.

They took their picture.

This is my favorite place.

Let's play together!

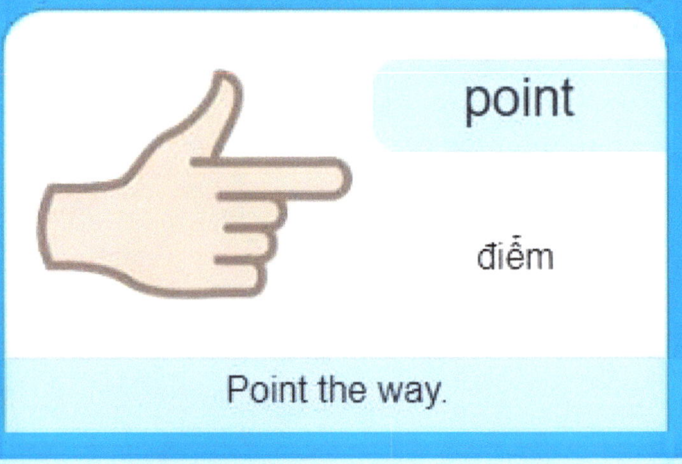

Point the way.

Please put the supplies away.

Do you like to read?

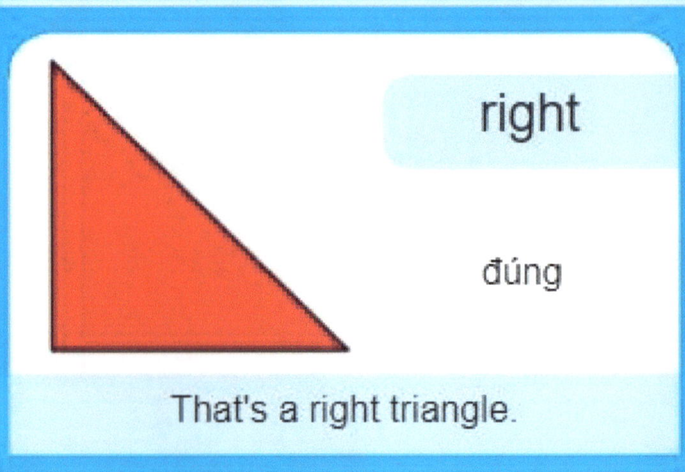

That's a right triangle.

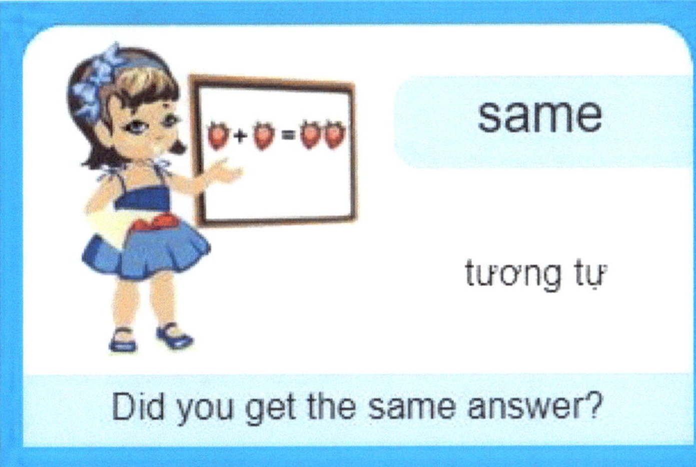

same

tương tự

Did you get the same answer?

say

nói

What did you say?

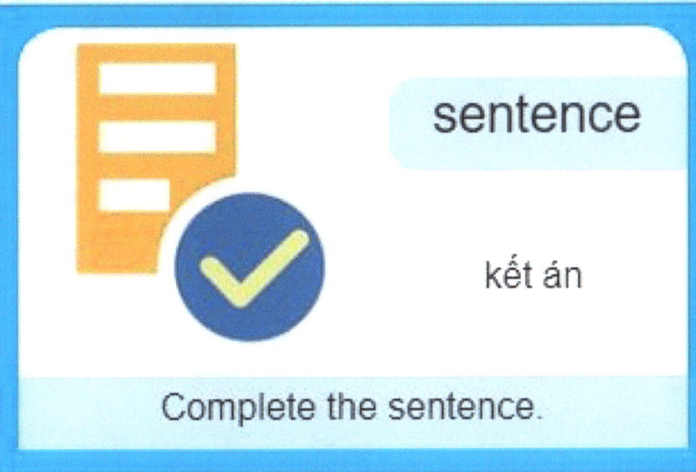

sentence

kết án

Complete the sentence.

set

bộ

Please set the table.

should

nên

We should exercise.

show

chỉ

Show your work.

small

nhỏ

The ladybug is small.

sound

âm thanh

A bee makes a buzzing sound.

spell

đánh vần

Please spell the word.

still

vẫn

I still want ice skates.

study

học

It's time to study.

such

như là

He is such a good dog.

take

lấy

Please take your seat.

tell

nói

She wanted to tell a secret.

things

nhiều thứ

She washed a lot of things.

think

suy nghĩ

Think about it.

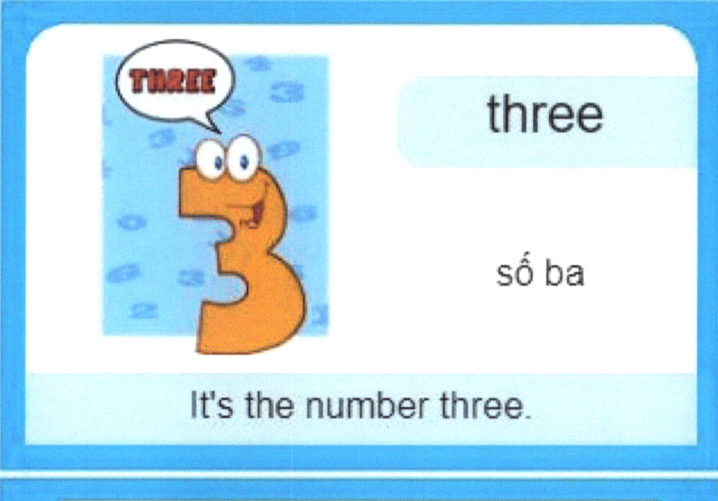

three

số ba

It's the number three.

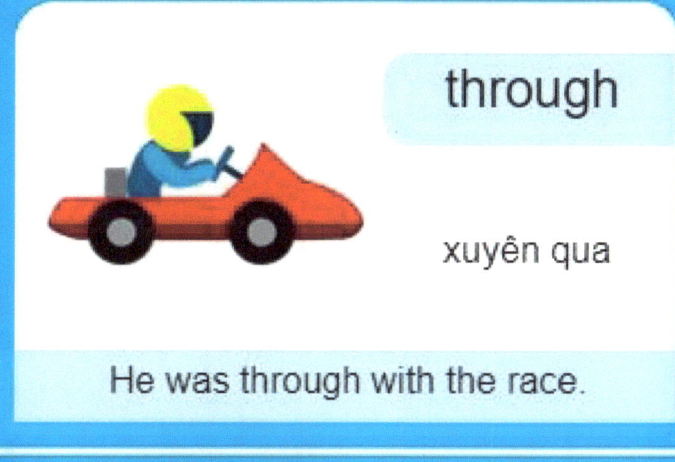

through

xuyên qua

He was through with the race.

too

quá

Do you like chocolate too?

try

thử

Try again, please.

turn

xoay

Turn in your homework.

us

chúng ta

She taught us.

very

rất

He is a very good singer.

want

muốn

I want to ride my bike.

well

tốt

You did well.

went

đã đi

We went to recess.

where

ở đâu

Where do you want to go?

why

tại sao

She asked why?

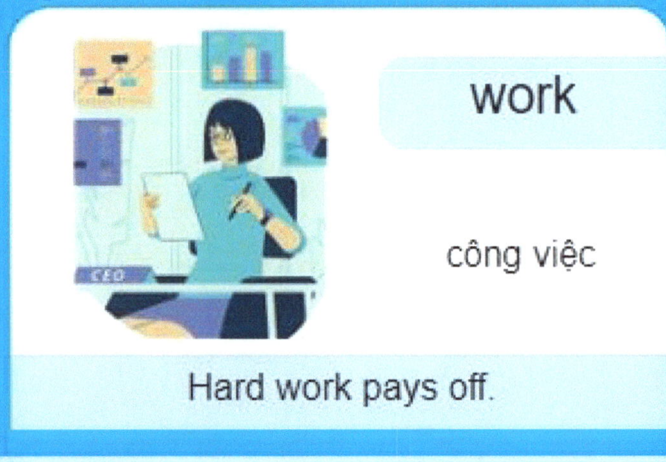

work

công việc

Hard work pays off.

world

thế giới

I want to travel the world.

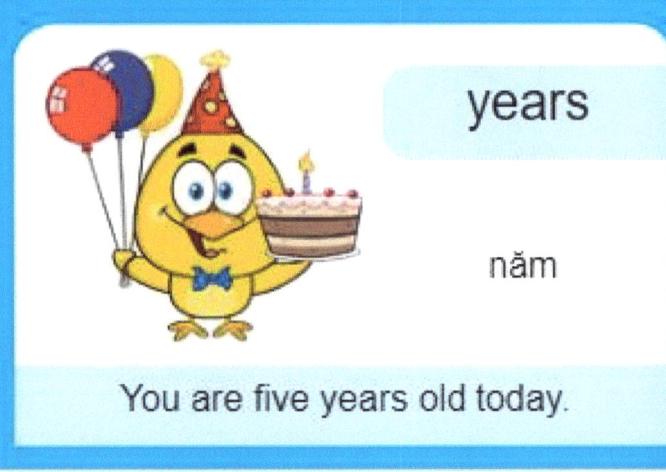

years

năm

You are five years old today.

above

ở trên

The sky was above them.

add

thêm vào

If you add one plus two, you get three.

almost

hầu hết

It's almost lunch time.

along

dọc theo

We get along.

always

luôn luôn

She always brushes her teeth.

began

đã bắt đầu

The baby began to cry.

begin

bắt đầu

You may begin your exam.

being

được

She is being shy.

below

phía dưới

It's below thirty degrees.

between

giữa

Two is between one and three.

book

sách

I'm reading this book.

both

cả hai

They both worked on math.

car

xe hơi

He bought a new car.

carry

mang

She had a bag to carry her groceries.

children

bọn trẻ

Four children sang.

city

thành phố

He worked in the city.

close

đóng

Please close the door.

country

quốc gia

Do you live in the country?

cut

cắt

You use scissors to cut.

don't

không phải

Don't forget!

earth

trái đất

Our planet is Earth.

eat

ăn

I eat bananas.

enough

đủ

Did you eat enough pancakes?

every

mỗi

I shower every day.

example

thí dụ

This is an example of a bird.

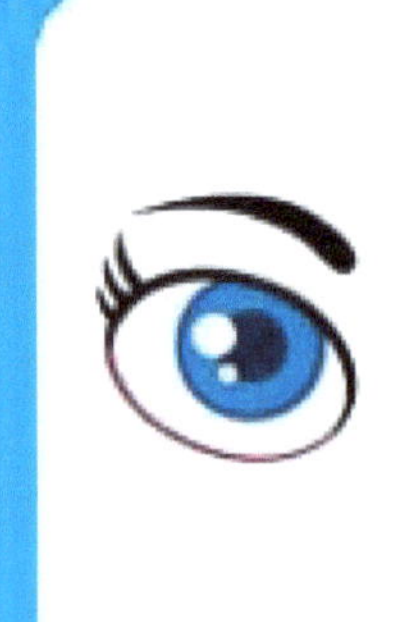

eyes

đôi mắt

What color are her eyes?

face

khuôn mặt

They were at the face painting booth.

family

gia đình

How big is your family?

far

xa

How far is it?

father

bố

Her father walked her to school.

feet

đôi chân

Put socks on your feet.

few

vài

She wanted a few more minutes.

food

món ăn

They made a lot of food.

four

bốn

There were four of them.

girl

con gái

The girl wore pink shoes.

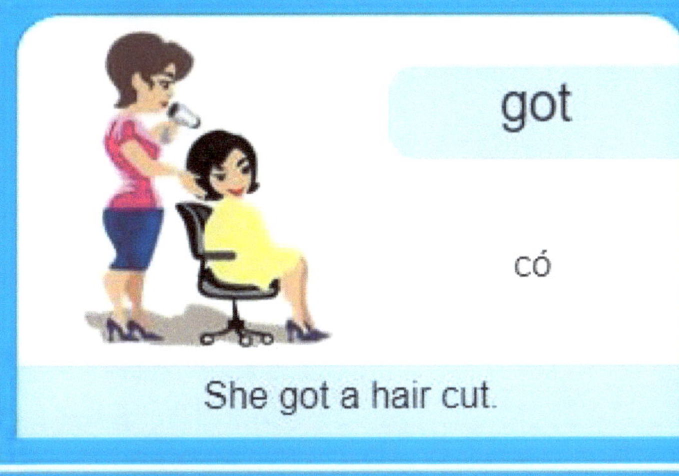

got

có

She got a hair cut.

group

nhóm

They were working in a group.

grow

lớn lên

The plant began to grow.

hard

cứng

He wore a hard hat.

head

cái đầu

He wore a cap on his head.

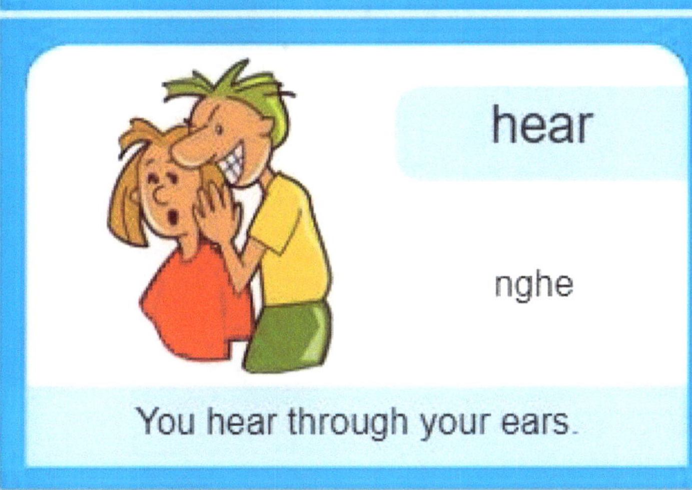

hear

nghe

You hear through your ears.

high

cao

She wore high heels.

idea

ý tưởng

I have an idea!

important

quan trọng

It's important!

Indian

người ấn độ

It's an Indian elephant.

it's

là

It's a tiger cub.

keep

giữ

Can you keep a secret?

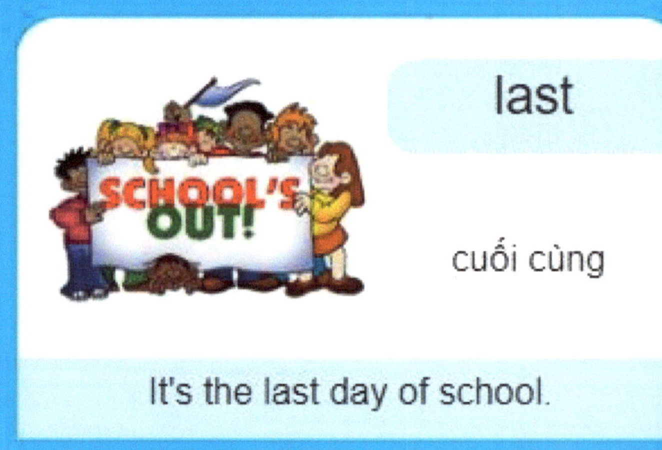

last

cuối cùng

It's the last day of school.

late

muộn

You're late.

leave

rời khỏi

He packed to leave.

left

trái

Are you left or right handed?

let

để cho

Will you let me go fishing?

life

đời sống

Life is about friends and family.

light

ánh sáng

The light turned yellow.

list

danh sách

Here's my to-do list

might

có thể

It might rain today.

mile

dặm

It's a mile from here.

miss

cô

You may correct any you miss.

mountains

núi

There are alot of mountains here.

near

ở gần

We are near the beach.

never

không bao giờ

I've never broken my leg.

next

kế tiếp

Take the next step.

night

đêm

You can see the stars at night.

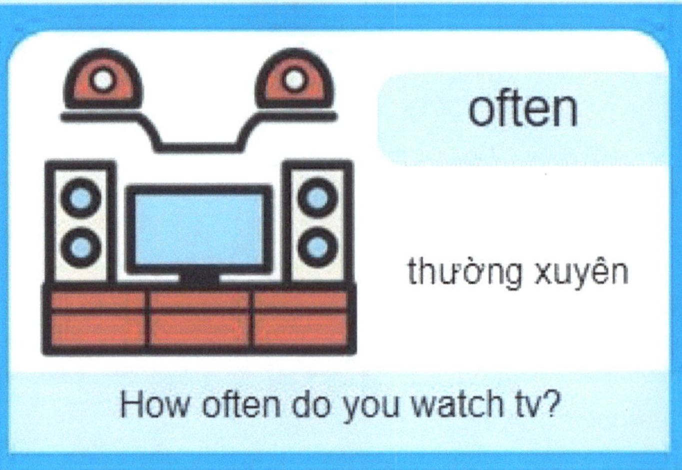

often

thường xuyên

How often do you watch tv?

once

một lần

Once upon a time…

open

mở

The door is open.

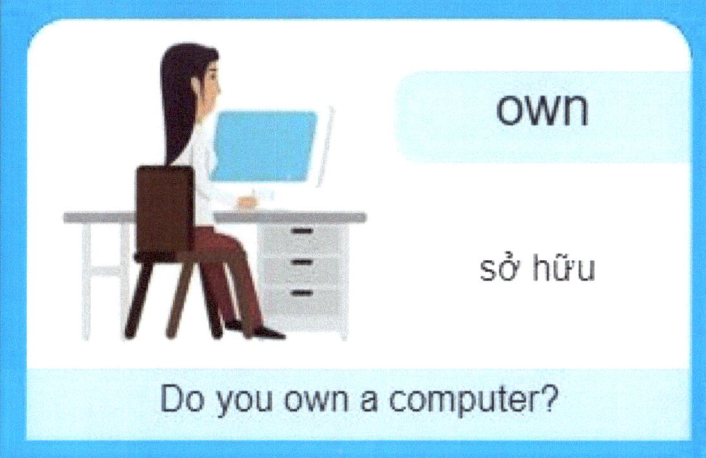

own

sở hữu

Do you own a computer?

paper

giấy

Do you have paper towels?

plant

cây

I will water the plant.

real

thực tế

Her real name is Sally.

river

con sông

The river is high.

run

chạy

He likes to run with his dog.

saw

xem

We saw a UFO.

school

trường học

Do you like school?

sea

biển

The ship is at sea.

second

thứ hai

She won second place.

seem

hình như

You seem busy.

side

bên

Each side of a square is the same.

something

một cái gì đó

Did you hear something?

sometimes

đôi khi

Sometimes we watch tv.

song

bài hát

We will sing a song.

soon

sớm

Dinner will be ready soon.

start

khởi đầu

Start writing.

state

tiểu bang

Which state do you live in?

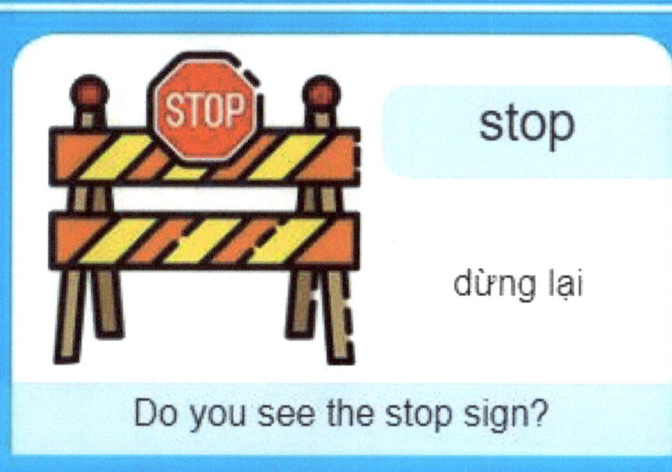

stop

dừng lại

Do you see the stop sign?

story

câu chuyện

What's the story about?

talk

nói chuyện

Let's talk.

those

những, cái đó

Those are great cookies!

thought

nghĩ

I thought the novel was good.

together

cùng với nhau

They went shopping together.

took

lấy

He took the last piece.

tree

cây

Did you decorate the tree?

under

dưới

It lives under the sea.

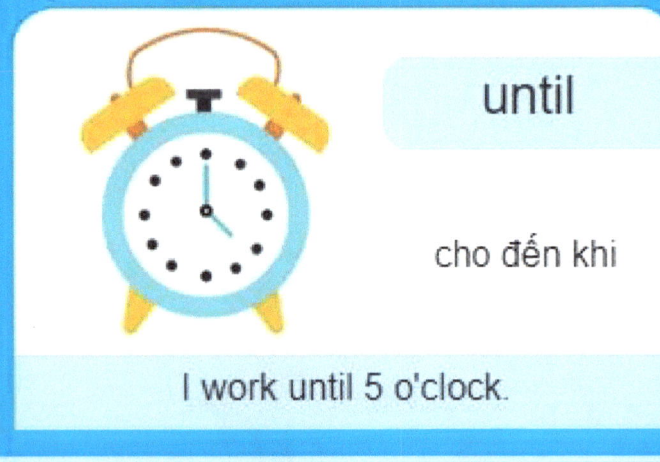

until

cho đến khi

I work until 5 o'clock.

walk

đi bộ

We went for a walk.

watch

đồng hồ đeo tay

Do you wear a watch?

while

trong khi

We had fun while skiing.

white

trắng

They drew on the white board.

without

không có

I can't go without my backpack.

young

trẻ

Her kids are young.

across

băng qua

It's across the street.

against

chống lại

It's against the rules.

area

khu vực

There are no wild animals in this area.

become

trở nên

It will become a butterfly.

best

tốt

Do your best!

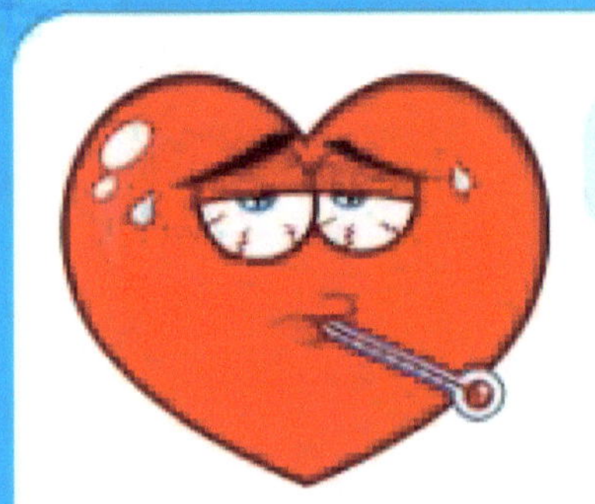

better

tốt hơn

Feel better soon!

birds

chim

There's a lot of birds.

black

đen

He has a black cat.

body

thân hình

The body has a lot of bones.

certain

nhất định

Certain words are harder than others.

cold

lạnh

It's cold outside.

color

màu sắc

What is your favorite color?

complete

hoàn thành

Did you complete your workout?